To These Dark Steps

By *Gabriel Levin*

POETRY

Sleepers of Beulah

Ostraca

The Maltese Dreambook

TRANSLATIONS

The Little Bookseller Oustaz Ali
by Ahmed Rassim

So What: New & Selected Poems 1971–2005
by Taha Muhammad Ali
(with Peter Cole and Yahya Hijazi)

Poems from the Diwan
by Yehuda Halevi

Gabriel Levin

To These Dark Steps

ANVIL PRESS POETRY

Published in 2012
by Anvil Press Poetry Ltd
Neptune House 70 Royal Hill London SE10 8RF
www.anvilpresspoetry.com

This book is published with financial assistance
from Arts Council England

Designed and set in Monotype Ehrhardt by Anvil
Printed and bound in Great Britain
by Hobbs the Printers Ltd

ISBN 978 0 85646 444 7

A catalogue record for this book
is available from the British Library

CONTENTS

ACKNOWLEDGEMENTS

Some of the poems in this collection originally
appeared in *Manhattan Review*, *PN Review*,
Raritan, the *Times Literary Supplement*, and
The Wolf.

A limited edition boxed set of twelve etchings
was created in 2011–12 by Ardyn Halter to
accompany the letterpress edition of Gabriel
Levin's sonnet corona *Wreath of Spume*. The
project was completed in March 2012 in an
edition of 18 signed copies with 4 artist proofs.
ardynket@netvision.net.il

The Hours a Traveler Measures

KOUROS

Blow after vertical blow severed you from the rock-face
in the abandoned quarry

the impact shatters the crystals deep inside you

and renders you opaque, lying there like a stunned space
    warrior,

oversized, grey-speckled feet pointing seaward
above the rooftops, while your double, sprawled in a grove

on the other side of the island, is having his torso

tickled by overhanging branches. – Imperturbable

youth, who once strode forward smiling, hands clenched
at your sides, undeterred, provides a seat

for the span of an hour. I hadn't realized the long descent

from the village-that-makes-verses on the mountain slope

would tire me so, leaning against your foursquare
frame, I doze, and wake, and doze again,

while the industrious ant, mistaking me for the figure

I've come to admire in its gritty silence, must about-face

as my right leg shudders and twitches involuntarily,
as if to say, behold the man.

THE HOURS A TRAVELER MEASURES

The Expedition

Confounded by the dark as I stepped out
of the station, I was bound to end up
walking in circles. The braided aerial roots
of a fichus called to mind black-figured youths
on Attic slipware, *the body is earth,*
but the mind is fire – grave-goods to cushion
the journey – so whose reverie had I entered anyway?

In the groggy morning. Porto Piccolo. A step
away from the Dogana. Via Malta. The hump-backed
bridge into the old town. "Even a paltry
thing is freighted with meaning if it flies
out of you." Before leaving
I'd jotted down: a quotation is not an excerpt.
A quotation is a cicada.

It was a bit of a scramble to reach
the bandy-legged god in his temple –
two pitted columns and a staved-in hut
on a spur beyond the tracks – but among citrus
in a gully I practically tripped over
these words in another tongue: ON THE GROUND
CHEERED BY THE SOUR ORANGE YOU'VE PICKED
THERE LIES THE HAPPINESS OF THE SOUL . . .

Archaic

There was always
    the promise, the finely
formed helix of the ear
    carved in coarse-
grained Anatolian
    marble: upright Young
Man in a Tunic – lean
    as any javelin
thrower, though thumb
    & forefinger at the waist
are all that's left of his severed
    arm: gazing across
the lagoon at the salt
    pans, the submerged
Punic road, leeward Tophet
    pits buried in myrtle.

The Poet Pines for his Homeland

'This was the place where Proserpina played'

In the last watch of the night, when the raven
flees the dove, Ibn Hamdis, itinerant,
poet-in-exile, set aside his panegyric – what child
of the Faith hasn't read his boasts? –
and hoisted the sail of his fancy
for the ruins of his native soil. – Oh Earthshaker,
you who hurled me beyond the Wandering
Rocks and obsidian flow of my desires . . .
Even as anguish stirred his soul
Ibn Hamdis couldn't help but polish the luster
of his lines, and snuffing the flame at his elbow
he was seized by the scent

of the fumitory that laced the island's
brambles, and he longed for its hinterland
and all the byways he'd tread with his father
under the sheer drops as the winds streamed
through the wild oat fields, and his heart went out
to its fabled haunt: how the low cries
in the rushes had shaken him to the core,
"Widgeon," his father whispered, "pochard,"
and his chest heaved like the earth itself
as the syllables rolled off the brackish waters,
and he croaked like a marsh toad
and knew himself not.

The Visit

By the time I'd covered the island
and reentered the city with its moldering
Palazzos, I was ready to slow down,
smiling as I pictured myself a month ago
    fresh off the plane, breaking up
                      the distances
in search of your whereabouts
– the perfect stranger abandoned
to alleys that bled into each other,
    tilting toward the port,
                  a force-field
shielding his anonymity – though now
it would be altogether different,
    sailing across town

to rest my eyes on you again
even as your own drift from the hand carved lectern,
distracted by what I take to be
a whirlwind visit beyond the frame
    where your glance falls
                and draws back
to the shadows of your own reserve,
casting in your mind the in–
conceivable,
    the eye can only go so far –
                while up close
the tiniest pit-holes appear in the glazing,
    the substance of your being   and gap
refusing to close where I freefall

GAZELLA, GAZELLA

The trail of serpent hues spools
out of the gully where a straw hat brightly
bobs its way home, everyone's got his point
of view, yours, however, is a sight to see – ground
into middle-earth pigments, light-wreathed,
fire-banked, the hills shift their bulk
at your touch – lapping our breath away

> *There were coordinates I couldn't imagine*
> *negotiating through the maquis,*
> *but the affection I felt for the swift-hoofed*
> *drove me on.*
> > *I bent over the last of the windflower*
> *petals, and the fire shifted hands.*
> *There was a fleetness in the air I just couldn't handle.*
> > *All five steadied their gaze*
> *at me within the circumspection of my binoculars,*
> *perdita perdita, predicated on the speed*
> *of their departure.*

it's as simple as that, like lisping trails
of clouds dispersing in the roadside puddle,
or opening the Book of Splendor onto
seven breaths (vanities) – but who was it last night
dropped such arcana into our laps? –
on which the world, or at the very least
your own firm ground stands clear.

GALILEAN ELEGIES

After the last scrape of the spade, he'd summoned
her back for us in the likes of the slip

of a girl she'd picture to him "before the bloody wars":
twiggy arms wrapped around her father's waist –

the good doctor on call, and she, in a pleated
skirt, astraddle the village donkey, clippedy-clop

on the healing path buried in wild mustard.
The anecdote stuck with us, the sun drove its nails

into the tableau. Years later, bent over the caper, I scratched
with a hand shovel around its root

in the gravelly soil, my fingers aching from the effort
to remove the spiny bush, *clippedy-clippedy-clop.*

*

The saga would begin here, where the Jordan tumbles
downward, turning on its bed to the bottom

of the world, a new life raveling out like the river
in its meanderings through the rift

in the valley *Lying there, gazing over the water*
That would have been the eldest son speaking,

stirring himself out of a reverie of origins,
boxed-in in the hill folds, the long, thermal corridor.

The yarn barely begun, pacing out the homestead,
the rock on which his head had rested

lugged a ways to mark the boundary line,
while high above wingspan and shadow amassing.

*

Rising from the schoolroom chair planted
between furrows in the stubble field, the accordionist

strapped his instrument shut, he's cradled
his last lullaby for the valley, while the women

beside him disperse, bearing the memory of melodies
    piped
carefree as wagtails, and now heaved from their chests,

in the faraway field accompanied by the old-timer's
arthritic chords, beyond the cowshed and defile

of cypress, beyond the prickly pear, the stricken field
that smelled of burnt trash and decomposing pelts,

the women in their batik floral patterns and billowy
pants disband. No more lullabies for the valley.

*

Remember the inflatable raft we'd brought
to the camp grounds north of Capernaum

where we'd pitched our pup tent and paddled out,
our sights on Tiberias, even as the wind blew us

off course and nearly drove us into Syrian waters.
How did we ever get out of such a fix? A covey of peacocks

squawking under the palm trees greeted our bungled
expedition, it had all seemed so easy, the squat basalt city

within a boy's reach, the following day we'd hike
to the Horns of Hittin. What did we know of defeat?

The sun burnishing the scimitar we'd coveted
in the market glanced off the miraculous waters.

                    *

By the end of the saga dreams chill the tongue
like crushed ice, children slake their thirst in the kiosk

before filing past the orange vest rerouting
traffic, you can stroll along the outer perimeters

of the defunct hydro-electric plant for a song;
where was it he'd stretched himself out, here or *here*,

by the rusty watchtower, the young idealist unloosed
in the pages piling up on your desk, years earlier

on your first visit to Palestine, rock and shale
welded into the form of a Golem *that hurried into life*

before his limbs were smooth, ungainly crows kick-boxing
in the parking lot, bold in their thigh feathers.

                    *

Unearthed combs, the dry, friable mound
rising over the tumbled bricks and ash of lives

you can hardly imagine – but the honeybees
perform their round or wagging Dance

as they once did for the man who'd stooped over
the clay and straw hives, wiping a band of sweat

from his brow like any day-laborer in the sun
on the slopes of a garrison town hard by the Jordan.

"And his eyes lit up," the locals might have said
of the harvester with his smoking brand. Scattered light

from the sky orienting the dancers home, pollen-
baskets attached to the hairs of their hind legs.

AUTO DA FÉ

Pressed for words panned
out in this rooftop

walk-up, this breathing
space where I suspend

my sentence, its clauses
hanging as unbarred light

prickles in, coaxes
one more confidence

no sooner said
denied, while wood

winds in zealous
hands grow musical

cresting above
the conservatory

– how the Castelo
shines on the hillside

smug as a buttercup
and how bravely

the caravel flaunts
its prow on the mantel

maritime dreams, Olá!
the pigeon gives me

its sidelong garnet–
in-the-eye look

while I lean over
the sill to greet the tram

clanking up the cobbles
so many faces flush

against the panes
What customs?

*What beliefs? Who is
their king?*

*

All night long the rain
drums its bull of pardon

suspended, renewed
over the dormer's brow

and smudges the open
ledgers of the lanes

below, *revise, revise*
and again, *revise*

it shushes in my ear
bookkeeper of diminishing

returns, though waxing
I self-divide

and each of my sundry
selves exacts its own

measure, zeros in
to the core

of the loving fire's light
at the far corner

of the west, Lady
da Luna, the pattering

rain knuckles me under
straight as a plumb

line, someone's softly
rapping at a door

as night raises its frayed
collar on the silver

screen of my fancy
– it's time, Lusus

to twine your thyrsus
cryptosemous

*

Hugging the noonday
hillside, cheek to abraded

jowl among griffin and angel-
heads with pilot wings

volutes and sirens licked
clean by the winds

I drag myself up
to the clock tower

hidden in plain
sight, chill shadow

in the square, tempo
passado fanning

the flames, skin
my words bare

as the fleabane poking
out of the culvert

confess, recant
to the chisel and mallet's

tinnitus, the tittle
and jot probing the fissures

and turned into a song
of sorts, *being nothing*

he was everything heard
from behind the painted

tower wrapped around
the scaffold

its mangled embrace
of granite and clock-face

waiting for its hour
to strike again

*

Belmonte

Follow the riverine
trees where the redstart

sings, follow the bend
follow the stalking crab spider

with bloated abdomen
on the petal, Oh errant

ingénieur des mines, follow
the scum, follow the mud

flats, follow the nests
of the little ringed plover

on the gravel depressions,
follow the shallows

and the unseen tattle
in the alders,

follow the square-rigged
vetchling in the viper

grass, follow the fly-
by-night toad "dissolving

in the element it knows
best," follow the call

of the blue rock thrush
(can you give me its

coordinates?) follow the spore
tufts lacing the tire-track

puddle, mining for tin
follow the underground seam

follow the lapidary
names, you who struck

a vein of song, insistent
doubled, clandestine

running uphill against
odds: revealed.

NORTH LIGHT

for J. F.

1. *How quietly he gave*

us the slip, he might have been
rounding a breakwater

as he lurched from kitchen
stool to sink: the prow

of his low-slung vessel
pitched in the brine, cranked

engines jiggling the flame
in the storm lantern.

2. *Did he burn his desires*

on the canvas,
and then walk under his own
ghoulish nightscapes?
The *Self-Portrait at Two A.M.*
gives me a chill, seeing him
there, about to escape
from his own desire to slap himself
down in the chair.

And there's the hour.
He can't sleep, but who can
under such conditions? Remember,
night doesn't fall here,
we can amble into it if we like,
but it's always just a step
ahead, outsmarting us.

I yearned to travel north,
as far as I could.
Imagined Lapland as just another
lambent landscape of his,
a twisted dream seized
and flattened out
for all of us to see.

I'd be like one of those Norwegian ships
following the trade winds.
Did he say that?

No, I didn't see the portrait
in Oslo,
but in a battered tome
with color plates
wrenched from a bookshelf.

We found forgotten parts of ourselves
like childhood names,
on every page,
and when not ourselves
the three sisters loomed out
of the lost surfaces.
Ah, Jen, he'd said, it's been
a long time. Slotted.
Sealed. Non-
pareil. *Forgive*
us.

3. *White nights*

we played murder
around the dining-room table.
One cries 'J'accuse,'
another turns his hand over
and falls silent. Night

makes itself scarce,
mislays its light swabs of dark
under our pillows. One
cries 'J'accuse,' another 'Innocent'
and a third turns his life over.

To These Dark Steps

NOW I BEHELD THE LIVING CREATURES

Little dustbowl brightly lit for Ramadan
with your peppermint minaret tops and cannon-fire,
greetings from an aging utopist, an orientalist manqué
on his evening jog along the path girding the Hill of Evil
     Counsel,
with its listing pine grove and its cyclamen, and burial
chambers buried in litter, *Ramadan karim*, I call out
to the fast-breaking family at their picnic table perched far
above their homes, heart pumping good-will,
my flared nostrils shrinking from the aroma
of skewered kebab, one more vanity of vanities;

could be they take me for another oddball from Am*ri*-ka
though this very morning I plugged into the kitchen
socket an electric cord slung across our courtyard
by a day-laborer from Jabel Mukkaber, and the construction
     site
next door lit up (did you know the word appears
in the O.T.: And out of the midst thereof
as the color of electrum) with activity and for the entire day
we grooved on one current, and when you moved,
I moved, like Ezekiel's wheels, but my endorphins
must have kicked in, for I'm thinking in contraries,

as I pound the old route wholly unknowable,
dear Sion, circling your bottomed out dustbowl,
your broke-backed roads and corrugated goat-sheds,
dear old Jabel, forgive us our follies. – *Yalla, urkod!*
a voice snaps at my heels, Come on, run! – Whereto?
I'm tempted to lob back, even as my Nikes bear me along,

hither, at nightfall, with this amalgam of gold
and silver some call electrum and others amber, and we,
out of the midst of the fire, its enfants terribles.

TO THESE DARK STEPS

Aerial Fire

Aza introduces a bright new face
   on the poetry scene, a native of Ashkelon,
the book in his hands is called *The Low*
   Table of Redemption, a clever turning on its head
of a Talmudic saying, all we desire
   of poetry is there in the exchange between Aza
and her soft-spoken guest, who'd rather read his poems
   than speak of their origins,
a faint tussle of paper can be heard

as we turn over the pages of the handout
   and follow the tilt of his voice, Tuesday, barely
a week into the New Year, and Y explains
   how *piguah*, which we hear as "terror attack," can mean
as well a simple, or less than simple encounter,
   as in "Jacob went on his way and angels of God
encountered him," but we suspect
   Y is toying with the fine line between meanings
as he reads on:

        round my body the scrolls are ablaze
        and hard by the café
        I stop in my tracks and gaze
        inhaling the aroma
        of dread and awe
        I seek a new covenant
        like the time I became a nation
        and noble

the skin on my face radiant
before I put on a veil and mask
I want to assail
it, to see the pavement
of sapphire
in the thunder and lightning of the heart

Back home, I've turned off the lights and all I hear
    is a procession of dark chords
in the opening measures of Coptic Light, woodwinds and
                                                    brass
    strings and vibraphones, a staggered, shimmering
weave, the hiss and dread assailing the ears
    of the undead, a complete twelve-tone chromatic
aerial bombardment, barely a week
    into the New Year, *Joy woke me up sobbing*
this morning, so what shall we do with this heart

turned into a wrecking ball,
    I asked what was the matter, nothing we can do
anything about, she replied, in the shock-and-awe of it all,
    Operation Cast Lead, operation toss
your hopes into the rubble of Jabaliya, I think of
Procopius
    of Gaza who wrote, "Amor and Amor's arrows
find their way everywhere," hadn't I dreamt
    of translating his overture – for he too
knew how in triumph we suffer defeat

After Webern

How to make sense of the unnerving
intervals played on the strings? And what if
the occluded cries rising from the debris
of our enmity
                  mix with the atonal world
I've ventured into? I've muted
the bows on the hi-fi, and in a little while
I'll have hammered myself

a sonnet-gone-awry that might
speak to our times. – Dear Anton, forgive me
for wrestling your broken, melodic
line to the ground this way,
                      but the skies, the skies
are pierced with wrath, as they would be
for you, stepping outside for air, the slug
spinning you to the dust.

Idée Fixe

By the 2nd movement you know it's not
going to stop. Inexorable. Meaning,
the music is settling old scores.
Nor is crying your eyes out
going to help. Snap.
Snap.
Snap.
Motivic. *What are you doing?*
What's that?
Take off those damn headphones.
There.
I'm listening to Bartok. Circa '39.
Why on earth.
I also like to listen in the morning to the birds
outside our window. Chirp. Chirp-chirp.
They too have a way of going on. *Yes, but.*
Over there. *Over where?*
Over there, hell with it, you know what I mean.
Pizzicato. Pizzicato. You pull at the strings
forcibly, and a city
crumbles, *pffff*. . .
Then silence.

Ground Offensive

Now it's Ligeti's turn, his black music
pulled over your face like a stocking in cutthroat
dread, and you make to reach out

and stop its advance but it slams you back
against the wall – this isn't what you wanted,
this is *agitato*, this is micropolyphonic,

as if you knew what that meant, but go on,
the Transylvanian child in you says: I'm your hostage,
let the alpenhorn sound its warning as white

phosphorus streaks the skies, tell me, what
has become of us, boom, boom, boom –
those are electrodes you took for earphones.

After Messiaen

Flame on the lamb's
back flickers in the candle-
holder and dies, solo
for clarinet, blackbird's
aubade, *Peep!* Eight move-
ments for the End of Time
and a wee heart in its rib
cage that beats faster

than its human complement,
Amor feathering through
the shoulder-blades,
breath spooled the length
of a wingspan. – In wooden
clogs and a patched up
suit off the back of a Czech
inmate, Messiaen

conducts his *Quartet*,
January 15, to a packed house
in Stalag VIII A, confined
to the monotony of barrack life,
how banish the temporal?
Subsisting on whale fat
and ersatz, and brutal sub-zero
temperatures, how

banish – if not for a satchel
of scores, and the *Imitation* –
winter of '41, once captured,

marched, transported, how then
unravel the tangled
ball of rhythms in your head
and go on? – Cross-legged
on my blue mat, fit as a fiddle

after yoking my body
to eight earthly postures,
equidistant from the speakers
from which the drawn out
tempo of the cello in the 5th
movement ripples across
the unlit room, midwinter,
mid-war, how compose

yourself, birdman, sound-
colorist? I draw in air,
slow, silent, easy, in what
I take as yogic harmony,
though not an easy task
with the Dance of Fury
pricking my ears, *compositeur
et rythmicien*, how, locked

behind prison camp doors,
usher in the celestial?
I fumble for the dials
to kill the hammer blows
and swelling sounds
and still the whirligig
in my head, the palin-
dromic raw war of the mind,

and the furies raging
in the skies, *perpetual motion
of steel*, how banish the un–
thinkable? Empty your
lungs, inhale, raise the chest
wall, hold, exhale – solo
for violin – picture wing-whirr,
the wee heart beating.

Melos

It's not as if the pages ruffled in the book
on your lap were blessing you with a many-headed
tune rippling through the thin bronze mouth-
piece of poetry: the eyeball Perseus snatched
from the Gray Ones might as well have been your own
groping effort to see more penetratingly.
The ring composition launches you on one escapade
after another, while hors text the sunbird hooks
its bill in the trumpet flower and tweets in the weed tree
shrilly, no less a feat than the sounds wrested
from the Gorgon's wail and tempered into polyphonic
song: rest assured, the gods will give one thing,

and another – *not yet*, the final, hanging clause
like any bird's rebuttal in the foliage,
or the DARK, EVERGLISTENING HUMAN EYES
your father encountered on the scorched roadside,
WE'VE SEEN THESE WRAITHS FLEEING . . . his fingers
     pounded
the keys no less fiercely than the gnashing jaws
of Medusa's sister. Some say Midas won the pipe-playing
contest for Akragas – splendor-loving polis,
Persephone's burrow – by persevering anyway
as his mouthpiece broke mid performance,
and egregious sounds wove a spell over the hearts
of the pastoralists milling on the high ground.

THE PITY WAR DISTILLED

Count the seasons in the blue armchair as the sun
beats softly through the panes and warms
my back before stepping outdoors to eye the wrong side up
rake that holds a drooping branch of the plum tree
at attention. Who can plumb the meaning of *huzn?* a friend
asks his Damascene friends. The veiled sadness
of the defeated, the sad pride of the baker at Zalatemo Sweets
as he rolls and flattens the cheese pastry. Airborne
seeds with feathery hairs light out to colonize new worlds,
wind-drift dispersed along the watershed –
Abu Tor, and beyond, Silwan, Bethany, and spiraling down,
down, to the Dead Sea. "Imagine the climate change,"
Halileh says, gazing at the Moab highlands
from Papa Andreas's rooftop terrace, "if the hills to the east
weren't so lofty." He fingers his cup, squints
at the ridgeline between domes.
                                        How he'd expounded
and danced around his own words as we shouldered
our way through the souk, the village boy from the Galilee
who'd gone up to university half a century ago
and faulted his teachers for their Arabic – *Sir, that's not a*
      house
but a fleet – returned home, snapped, and mended,
and taught, and snapped again: was it the fire-born djinn
or the Security Services that dogged
his every step, stringing his wife and children along,
even his dearest brother now in the grave?
"And still I wouldn't break" he tells me
through his clenched gold teeth. I fetch from my bag

the outcast Shanfara's "Arabian Ode in the Letter
L," "That's me," he exclaims, pointing to the open page:
the noble-hearted, adrift in this land, seeking
refuge from insult and injury, drifts further afield.

THE WEIGHING OF SOULS

What of the anonymous faces poking
out of the antique masonry? *Gislebertus made
this* – carved heads with broad, shapeless snouts,
grimacing from their chinks and sooty
vaults. Why is it, with their bulging brows
and sunken, bandito eyes, their huge,
gaping mouths and devilish looks
(last night, muting the newscast,
I read in *Imago Hominis* such masks
were the face of evil) why then is it they evoke,
the evident . . . no, the risibly human?
However twisted their features, we trip over
our own shadows in the dissembler,
the suicide and the buffoon, the bold warrior
and the sinner on the pan of the scales.

THE FATHERS ARE WATCHING

I beat a retreat but the retreat hits back and when I'm flat out it pours a bucketful of arpeggios to revive my sullen disbelief. Hey, what's going on, I cry out, coming to. – Relax, and face the music.

When Zeus thunders the Muses slip away to their favorite swimming hole, dipping their toes into Helicon's waters as they gaze at the heavens' reflection, determined to pick out Orpheus's Lyre. Why should Zeus have such an effect on his daughters who trip on soft feet? Are they merely "lily-voiced," insouciant, distractible, and, at best, of two minds, not unlike the sleeping shepherds on the watch they so fondly like to prod into song? Is this not the meaning of their very first words: Meadowland shepherds, wretched things of shame, mere bellies, we know how to speak many falsehoods as though they were true, but we know, when we wish, how to say the truth.

*

A chopper circles the Dome of the Rock like a mule harnessed to a water wheel. Achmed, his trowel caked with mortar, shifts his gaze from the runaway wall to the whirling rotors. Snug in the cockpit Moshe nudges his co-pilot. His partner stares down through his field glasses and splits his sides laughing, and the two break into song, *the floods stood straight like a wall / the deeps froze in the heart of the sea.* A very ancient song, but for them just words sung cunningly on their lip. And what could the Sages have possibly meant by: Where is a man's heart located? Two-thirds of the way up from the soles of their feet. So He

congealed the Sea about them to two-thirds of its depth.
This is all puzzling: are we rising or sinking? I'd rather
quote a little poem by Brecht called "The Trowel" which
appears rather ominously before the equally short "The
Muses" in my English edition of his poems.

> In a dream I stood on a building site. I was
> A bricklayer. In my hand
> I held a trowel. But when I bent down
> For mortar, a shot rang out
> That tore half the iron
> Off my trowel.

*

Our heads reeled at the sight of the funambulist as he
gripped his balancing pole over the Valley of Judgment. All
the little devils clutched their parents' hands in dread.
Would he ever make it to the other side? Midway, sus-
pended over the pyramidal roof of Absalom's Tomb splat-
tered with pigeon droppings, he seemed to forget from
what side he had set out in the first place. Forward! No,
back, back! The crowd shouted. Poor transfixed soul, deaf
to our entreaties. Even his manager with the shining bull-
horn can't get him to budge. Then the ring-necked parrot
arrived sheathed in its green kimono. It had long replaced
the hoopoe as the cleverest, if not the wisest of birds. You
could see the arriviste lording it in the tallest, weariest
branches of the eucalyptus – also an import – from Dan to
Beer-Sheba. Alighting on the funambulist's shoulder, it let
out such a squawk, his ear instantly unplugged and he slid
down the auditory canal all the way to China. Young and
old were delighted by his vanishing act. Some loitered in
the valley, others wound their way to catch a matinée at the

cinematheque, which as everybody knows is built on the slopes of Gehenna.

*

Once on reserve duty in the Jordan Rift Valley – this must have been in the mid-eighties – a soldier in ill-fitting khakis told me he'd flung his drums into the Dead Sea. He'd looked so young and dreamy. At first I thought he'd said teddy bears (*doobim* in Hebrew) and not drums (*toopim*). But no. He'd played in a rock band before his induction and had been allowed to rehearse on the base when off duty. And yet his playing rang hollow in the recreation room. He couldn't help feeling he was betraying the rhythms that had kept him whole in his youth. I had imagined I could shake off my youthful self, he told me, by hurling into the sea my drums, but instead I'm sinking fast into a void of my own making. Without music, I'm nothing. I looked into his eyes and believed I saw the Demon of Analogy lurking dimly in the depth of his pupils. I myself had only recently read of this strangest of creatures and its restless traffic between unlikely signs. Would it come to the boy's rescue at the penultimate hour as we stamped our boots listlessly in the dusty outpost?

*

Why would Athena have insisted imitating on the double flute the sounds of the dreadful Gorgons as they gnashed and wailed at the fate of their sister whose severed head Perseus held in his upraised hand? Pindar tells us Athena named the melody "many-headed" – perhaps in memory of the snakes coiled in their hair – and promptly handed the tune over to mortals. Gray-eyed Athena clearly sympathized

49

with the sisters and immortalized their anguish by invent-
ing a tune that sounded more like the skirl of a bagpipe than
the strum of a lyre. It was she, after all, who turned the
irresistible maidens into such monsters after Poseidon
ravished Medusa in Athena's own temple. How easily the
gods turn a beautiful, venerated object into its opposite. A
late scholia to Pythian 12 informs the reader, however, that
the victor in the flute competition may have won by blowing
through a broken mouthpiece that had produced discordant
yet utterly captivating sounds.

*

How many times had I attempted reading *The Groundwork*
and failed? And yet I was convinced it held the key to
human rectitude. Only yesterday I imagined thrusting a
copy of the book into the hands of one of the soldiers who
had swooped down on us in a hummer south of Hebron.
Here, read this, I fancied telling him, but then I pictured
the fellow, loaded down with tear-gas canisters, asking why
he should bother reading that sort of stuff. How was I to
defend a book which I hadn't been able to finish? Instead I
pointed to the donkey on the ridge above us and said: I
wonder what he must think of the fuss we're making at the
bottom of this forlorn valley? The combatant looked up
and muttered something about how the locals mistreat their
beasts of burden. Later in the day, after we had grown
weary of facing each other in the sweltering heat, and were
about to disperse, the donkey wove a headstrong path down
the slope, its burly rider swatting the animal's flanks with a
stick and singing a saucy little song in Arabic. I didn't quite
catch the words, but for some reason was reminded of
Balaam's talking ass and an ancient midrashic text came to
mind: At first the ass alone perceived the angel and not

Balaam. This was God's doing – so goes the homily – for He understood that should man perceive the angels, surrounding him, he would surely lose his mind in terror.

*

Is it true the Muses stripped the Sirens of their feathers, which they then plaited into crowns after trouncing the bird-women in a musical contest? A plucked bird isn't a pretty sight. The dreaded Sirens had once been Kore's play-mates, bewitched, some say, by Demeter who gave them wings and told them to set out in search of her daughter. Whatever the case, the Argo sailed into view and the Sirens, delighted at the prospect of the pick of the Greek beau monde, broke into the most ravishing of strains as they stepped over the bones of their former victims. Little did they suspect that Orpheus was on board. He grabbed his lyre and in lightning rhythms drowned out the Sirens' "high clear call." Twice, thrice defeated, the bird-women contemplated suicide. But they were still there when Odysseus rounded the cape. Their voices pitched to the atonality of a ravaged world.

*

I was listening to Webern. Three Pieces for String Quartet. Vocals beginning, *Grief always / looking upward*. Its length barely two and a half minutes, the same amount of time it would take our fighter jets (when I was a child they were called *Phantoms*) to take off, drop their deadly load, and return home. How proudly we tapped the glass casing of our watches: 2 min and 32 sec. I bend forward in my chair, press Repeat, adjust my earphones. Diminishing half-tones spun in a centrifuge. Elsewhere the body count begins.

Schmerz, immer / Blick nach oben. Elsewhere people sift through debris for their dear ones. When I've tired of Webern I reach for S.Y. Agnon's "At the Onset of the Day," the same conciseness, the same brevity transposed into words, the same otherworldliness rising from and sinking into chaos, the *tohu-bohu* of Genesis. "After the enemy destroyed my home," so begins Agnon's short tale of moral and physical devastation, "I took my little daughter in my arms and fled with her to the city." The *Book of Splendor* speaks of darkness giving strength to *tohu* while "Spirit is the voice that dwells with *bohu*." But we live in benighted times and even the sky menaces and is no longer a place of refuge, as in Dennis Silk's mid-80s Stingy Kids sequence on "the situation" (Hebrew *ha'matzav*: the anesthetizing catch-all phrase commonly used in speaking of the century-old deadlock): "Sky's legal, reached by a staircase. Up here, at least a floor higher than the troops." Silk, the most private of poets, apprenticing himself "to a horse laugh" in dire times:

In this fable by Aesop, men manage to become birds. They salute each other across little parcels of air. Space be about you, Marwan.' 'Redoubled space be about you, Raja.'

*

We drove north to the Hula swamps for a weekend of bird watching. What is now called the Little Hula Lake was once a vast swampland in the middle of the panhandle. Who hasn't heard of the malarial swamps and the valiant settlers of the State-in-the-making who drained them dry to rid the area of the anopheles mosquito and provide large tracts of arable land? By the nineties, however, the rapidly vanishing wildlife and once-fertile peat soils turning into black dust, environmentalists finally convinced the authorities to reflood parts of the valley. Just before the turnoff to the village where we've rented a cabin I notice a sign pointing to *Khirbet Yarda* at the end of a winding dirt road. "I'm in Yarda on the fishbanks of the Jordan," wrote Yeshurun in a poem I had translated some years back, "We overran its homes (the fact is our life). / Returned to dust, spare us." This must have been during the '48 war. The poet had served in the infantry on the Syrian border. Witnessing the exodus of the fellahin of Yarda and neighboring Dardara, made him change his name from Yechiel Perlmutter to Avot Yeshurun, meaning The Fathers Are Watching. The next day I locate Dardara, now picnic grounds east of the Jordan. Little more than a Bedouin encampment, it was fated to be shelled by both Syria and Israel:

> At daybreak Yarda was plowed over,
> Dumb witnesses yonder fish.
> All night we called out Dardara, Dardara.
> Our voices sank in the Little Hula Lake.

When we finally do pedal around the lake I catch sight of a marsh harrier slow-circling above the papyrus reeds. And the young nature guide at one of the lookout posts explains, training her telescope on a flock of migratory cranes, that their bugle call – reveille at dawn? – is due to their enlarged windpipes, coiling like the bends of the Jordan.

*

The little man in the silk yarmulke who accepted the Nobel Prize for literature in Stockholm in 1966 was undoubtedly visited by a demon. Or daemon. S. Y. Agnon is described somewhere as a young man lying on the floor stark naked in his room in Ottoman Jaffa reading a heavy-set folio edition of the Talmud. His adopted name loosely meaning "separated souls," born in the Galician town of Buczacz to a family with the name of Czaczkes, Agnon reveled in unlikely correspondences, or those that misfire. Father and daughter seek refuge in the courtyard of the Great Synagogue in the father's home town. It is the eve of the Day of Atonement and as she warms her hands over the memorial candle the girl's dress catches fire. "We had fled in panic, destruction at our heels, and had taken nothing with us. Now that fire had consumed her dress, I had nothing with which to cover my daughter." With increasing pain and anguish the narrator of "At the Outset of the Day" sets forth in vain to find his daughter a garment to cover her naked body. Even the Geniza or storeroom for discarded scraps of writing in Hebrew, "where in my youth I had found among the written shreds, wondrous and amazing things," fails to provide him with the flimsiest of coverings. Read as the figure of the soul (*neshama* in Hebrew), the Daughter of Israel, shivering in the cold light, can no longer be protected by the signs – the sacred writings – of a lost world. It would take, once again, a daemon to see the correspondences between the catastrophic past and the youthful, heady days of early statehood – with their own moral malaise – when Agnon penned the parable (described with typical self-irony as "A simple and straightforward affair") in his study on the outskirts of the city from where, climbing to the rooftop of his home, he could catch a glimpse of the Dead Sea.

*

Dabeah, Arabic for hyena. Rural Ottoman and Mandate Palestine once teemed with such bone-crunching scavengers, their sinister, high-pitched laugh, eerily human, heard on the outskirts of villages at nightfall – may have enthralled like the song of the Sirens. So many villages emptied and razed to the ground, but the *dabeah* abounds in the imagination of the fellahin who remained and whose villages have grown into sprawling towns on the slopes of the Little Triangle in the lower Galilee. Like little Aref Attala who strayed from Sultan's Road in the pre-dawn hours and was accosted by "something black as the wind" that lurched at him and stuck one paw on his left shoulder and another on his right and pressed its mouth against his mouth and its eyes against his eyes and then opened its mouth wide and shrieked, and the boy lost his mind and chased after the hyena, crying out: Ya'ba [father], wait for me, stop, Ya'ba, stop. Such was the allure of the perilous. And even when the mighty el-Hajj Ali heard the boy shouting and galloped on his newly-shod horse, sparks flying in all directions, and caught up with the boy and seized hold of him, Attala tried to free himself from his grip and cried out: Let go of me! I want to reach my father. And not before el-Hajj Ali picked up a rock and struck the boy's forehead and drew blood was Attala cured. For whoever is under the spell of a hyena cannot be healed – so ends the tale – without the drawing of blood.

*

"When the man of iron beats them / the Muses sing louder." The companion piece to "The Trowel" reverses the saying "when the cannons thunder the Muses are silent," calling attention to our own covert pleasure – "with blackened eyes / they adore him like bitches" – our own coy submissiveness to the powers that be in mean-spirited times: "Their buttocks twitch with pain. / Their thighs with lust." The Muses belong to an unbending social order, and sing, as Hesiod would have it, with consenting voice, they are of one mind, *homophronas*. Perhaps this is why they are nine; a tenth Muse would carry them out of the cozy family network of primary numbers into multiplicity, duplication, iteration, the "many-headed." She would belong to a world of misrule and might be called – to borrow a phrase of Brodsky's – a Keening Muse: for she keens like mothers keen for the fallen. (She also pilfers and trespasses, Hermes her tutelary spirit.) She is dodecaphonic. "All of its beauty," writes Adorno of modern music, "is in denying itself the illusion of beauty." She brays inelegantly like an ass. The strings of her lyre cut into her fingers. She snarls looking skyward as she sinks.

AS I STOOD

Saul Tchernichowsky

Soul-voice sheathed in light, errant-voice
   in foreign darkness jostle within me, as a rule
   unblessed, I'm hemmed in by qualms, doubtful
fervor twists my dreams into boisterous

upheavals, where the living cling to
   each verdict-piercing sentence, chipping away
   at *Shaddai*, my badge of good faith pinned to gray
fatigues, of common places none, or few

were left to me: nothing but crumbling clots
of earth, chaff borne in a swelter of barn lofts,
   spade-clink in furrow, sickle in grain shrill,

village-rapt, unfettered in my seedtime – who
stood by me in grief, in battle and heart-rue,
   as I stood between the living and the still?

*

As I stood between the living and the still
   dying (how awful a craft!) scalpel in the palm
   of my hand, weeping for joy, cursing in alarm,
I absorbed the dying light from the pupil

of a stranger, while cannon thundered in the plain,
   and a flame sputtered in the gloom of the trench
   for me alone: I drew the last line, wrenched
the living from my page, the way a gem is plucked

from an onyx bowl – and yet in the very glitter
   in the dim eye, in light absorbing light, before rising
everlastingly, in the searing flash of fire,

   in fire that summons fire, bidding disaster – abiding
within, your glory stunned me – had I come too
soon, or was the Rock, my creator, overdue?

Wreath of Spume

WREATH OF SPUME

'How came we ashore?'

Not the beacon taking its own sweet time –
    on-off, on-off at the count of four under
    my breath, rounding the Cape of Wonder –
nor these words barely spoken and hardly mine
flung back unstitched out of the brine
    dispel the unease, choppy seas, November
    winds, throbbing engines, muffled thunder; –
here's a colloquy of sorts to divine,
a backtracking and forward voice with nowhere
to go, I practically fall over the chair
    bolted to the deck, bruise my knee, what's more
    the pilot sweeps his search light for –
not *I* – the providential fall. Blindsided,
have you seen a single thing better guided?

Have you seen a single thing better guided
    in its ignorance than my own heaven-
    bound reading? Once, twice, the child I'd been
looked up and felt himself undivided
from the vast, interstellar space
    above; now though it's time to retire
    down corridors, rubbing shoulders with fire-
extinguishers – kind keepers – securely in place.
It's a snug home, this berth, this orgone box
of mine, I even have my own code to fox
    me into my lair, with neat gadgets delighted
to entertain my errant mind: insistent,
flickering, on the run, already distant,
    by its own light on the dark cape sighted.

By its own light on the dark cape sighted,
    we're running the length of the spectral
    island, landforms, barely picked out, a scrawl
of pre-dawn wattage, low, constant, blighted
micro-transmissions on the benighted
    mountain flanks, opaque gestural
    sweeps of a tarred brush yield to the lustral
silvering of the east: you almost feel chided
while the ship's intercom broadcasts landfall
to the fast asleep. We veer at a crawl
    into port. Battlement walls, a ruined tower,
the rest is a blur. Not even the chime
    of bells sets you aright, alert to the hour,
nor your hand sweeping the grass for a rhyme.

. . . Nor your hand sweeping the grass for a rhyme
    can fill the blank, the hanging phrase and repose
    begun further back than you'll ever suppose,
mid-sentence, mid-flight, the scent of thyme
in word-joints, the first avowal;
    shoot of a man who walks the coastline
    ready to combust, ready to dance on a dime
at every turn of the road, the stretch of a vowel
his tinder. Scrub oak, woodsmoke, the quicksilver
    underleaf of the olive. Gray, toothed peaks beyond
    his reach. A feral place he might grow fond
of, even with its boar foraging the interior.
    but can any sort of paraphrasing
    parse the phrase that bears rephrasing?

Parse the phrase that bears rephrasing
    if you can. It's a tease to say the coast is clear,
    but who's faulting you for trying: a belvedere
to look out from, the eye appraising
ripple and wrack, the constant replaying
    of riptide as the cloud-shifting, sheer
    Veronese skies transport me to the dear
crystal troposphere and replenishing
azure. "Wrap yourself in the vanishing wisps
of clouds," reads The Book of Ambling, "in slips
    of grass," even as darker shades of cumuli
    roll in, giving off the strangest light – dry,
fierce, portentous, penetrating from afar.
What is it you hear whispered, *outrenoire*.

What is it you hear whispered, outrenoire,
     outremer, outretombe, beyond the black
     and the sea and the grave – in extremis – the rack
and ruin of the near at hand, the *you can only go so far*
in the why and wherefrom: starlings scrape
     the treeline, black on white, a shrill
     inky song, that rattles and loosens the nil,
the naught in the binding. How the mountains drape
the island in verdigris of darkest green.
Nightfall, all is guesswork, sleuthwork, the unseen
     life, the cracked masonry, the wrecked car
in the yard, men in camouflage slipping out
for the hunt – they'll tell you what it's all about,
     sounds escaping under a jester's cap jar.

Sounds escaping under a jester's cap jar
    and prick the senses. What makes you believe
    you can take it all in? The turbulent sleeve
of freshwater and sea-marge, a sand-bar,
quaking grass, landing strip, bamboo mist, scar-
    faced schist, looked at hard enough undeceive
    the mind otherwise porous as a sieve.
Molten, shoot of a man, is this who you are?
Consider Tchernichowsky on the Black Sea,
    1919. *Soul-voice sheathed in light, errant-voice*
in foreign darkness jostle within me.
    Hebraist, Russo-Levanter, another choice
phantasm to contend with, word-blazing,
the spinner of yarns, nothing short of amazing.

The spinner of yarns, nothing short of amazing,
    now Astarte addressing, and now the flesh
    of a mosquito sung in the glow and mesh,
the tongue's pearl and peril – a maze to sing
from; I thought I heard a suspiration
    in the hawsers, infinitesimal
    soundings plumbed where the low-slung *Squall*
and *l'Espérance* rocked in suasion
as I walked that morning the dockside.
    It was a thing of the air provoked the brain
    to unclench in the port of . . . but why give the name
away? All I heard was the listing *abide*
    of the masts: the clock was ticking, in sum.
    One more night crossing, one more periplum.

One more night crossing, one more periplum,
   one more goatpath scramble, one more specimen
   plucked for the satchel, one more toponymn
unremembered, one more specter to run
into: companionable other, hum–
   drum intimation, like the feldspar glint
   in the mason's eye that cozens you into the Flint-
stone Age; another voyage clocked from
Else to Where. Anything can happen here
on the island. Someone shouts All clear
   and then, crack! a round of shots leads
you to an old quarry, a firing range,
the register of low tones, a clipped exchange
   for the books that speak to you of strange deeds.

For the books that speak to you of strange deeds
    I propose these misadventures. The gloss
    where the water fumbles and retreats, cross–
currents in the estuary, conspiratorial reeds.
This could make for a cloak–and–dagger sub-
    plot to follow up on. The searchlight combing
    the sea. Remember? The boar–head gloaming
the wall of the tavern. The stub
and stumble of tongues, phrases dressed down
in motley, the jester's cap and frown
    on the bag-lady accosting, "Where d'you comes
from?" Rounding a corner, in miserable
    weather, "the mountains?" Words, crumbs
cast in the spindrift along the littoral.

Cast in the spindrift along the littoral
    I thought I'd never set my feet down again
    on solid ground, it was all in the bargain
I hadn't seen coming, the sudden figural
sweep in the hidden design, the conjectural
    dream, the traction, forever uncertain,
    and disclosure, when the vaporous curtain
rises, a docu-drama, an unreeling pastoral
underwritten and scored by the clamor
of its vanishing. Vamoose, says the charmer
    of serpents, and the chimera coils back
    to the bottomless bottom of the sack.
So I drifted along the seaboard and spun
east to west and back ever and anon.

East to west and back ever and anon,
　　the shoot of a man on the winding will
　　of a road, leaving behind bathers still
wading into a lake, foliage begun
to turn, stately homes, a temple, a distant
　　cascade, and in the middle ground the tip
　　of the brush has seized upon a bit
of rustic scenery: a soft, deliquescent
scene, three figures reclining at the edge
of a grotto, staring from their vantage
　　at the foregrounded youth on his knees
cupping water in his hands, while the stoop
of a man stops in his tracks, follows suit,
　　borne to the verge where no one heeds . . .

Borne to the verge where no one heeds
    the raptor's scare-notes, bend over to drink from
    the springs, the brooks and rivulets that run
and vein the mountains and idle by the reeds
shadowing the wetlands, stoop, quaff
    your brew at the source that foams and wells
    at your feet, the island casting its spells
has had its way with you, leaving the chaff
behind, the pronominal resolve,
    you and *I*, and the shoot – or was it the stoop? –
of a man in mid-stride seeming integral
    to the picture beginning to dissolve
as lightning, thunder, cloudburst, recoup
    the signs: strong winds, out of the temporal.

The signs: strong winds, out of the temporal
    turned into tempest music, goat-horn
    fife and reed, and songsters I can hear
circling, "We thought ourselves at a carnival"
cantu, incantu for three voices to marvel
    at – a spray, a wreath of spume to adorn
    the islanders with, anything that might cheer
me up as I prepare to leave and a liberal
peal of bells resounds from the ferry.
All lit up, she might as well be the Faerie
    Queene awaiting my arrival, one more
    fantastical tale, one more song to store
for keeps that hasn't lost its shine,
not the beacon taking its own sweet time.

Not the beacon taking its own sweet time –
have you seen a single thing better guided
by its own light on the dark cape sighted? –
nor your hand sweeping the grass for a rhyme
parse the phrase that bears rephrasing.
What is it you hear whispered outrenoire,
sounds escaping under a jester's cap jar
the spinner of yarns, nothing short of amazing,
one more night crossing, one more periplum,
for the books that speak to you of strange deeds
cast in the spindrift along the littoral,
east to west and back ever and anon
borne to the verge where no one heeds
the signs: strong winds out of the temporal.

NOTES

THE EXPEDITION

The Poet Pines for his Homeland (p. 14)

Abd al-Jabbar Ibn Hamdis left his native Sicily in 1078 at the age of twenty-four, and for the rest of his long life wandered in al-Andalus and North Africa as a court poet, singing the praises of his Arab hosts and lamenting the loss of his home and the demise of Muslim culture in the wake of the Norman invasion of Sicily and the Reconquista in Spain.

AUTO DA FÉ (p. 23)

the loving fire's light: João Pinto Delgado.

ingénieur des mines: born in Poland in 1880, Samuel Schwarz studied mining engineering in Paris at the turn of the century and after working as an engineer in Russia, Poland, England, the Ivory Coast, Galicia, and Italy, finally settled in Portugal in 1915. It was while mining in the region of Belmonte that he encountered small, clandestine communities of Marranos (otherwise known as Conversos, New Christians, or Crypto-Jews), Christians on the outside, while inwardly clinging to vestiges of Jewish prayer and ritual. In 1926 Schwarz published in Portuguese the first study of the Marranos, consisting largely of their religious hymns, which for centuries had been handed down orally from mother to daughter.

AERIAL FIRE (pp. 35–36)

Lines 19–32: "round my body the scrolls . . . lightning of the heart" is translated from the Hebrew of Yoram Nissinovitch.

THE PITY WAR DISTILLED (p. 45)

"Arabian Ode in the Letter L": *Lamiyyat al-Arab*, the title conferred to one of the most famous, pre-Islamic qasidas, monorhymed in the letter *lam*, or "l" and attributed to the legendary brigand-poet and outcast, al-Shanfara of the tribe of Azd.

Saul Tchernichowsky (1875–1943), who was born in the southern Ukraine and saw considerable frontline action as an army doctor throughout World War I, was considered the most versatile and sun-intoxicated (nicknamed "the salted Greek" in his native Mikailovka) myth-maker of the poets of the Hebrew cultural revival at the turn of the 20th century. He was also an indefatigable translator, notably from the Greek. He managed to leave Soviet Russia in 1922 and lived in Berlin for nine years before settling in Tel Aviv together with his Russian Orthodox wife.

"As I Stood" renders into English the sixth and seventh sonnets in the poet's Corona of Sonnets "To the Sun," written in Hebrew in Odessa in 1919. Originating in the Italian Renaissance, the intricate, fifteen-sonnet form had been adapted by a number of Russian Symbolist poets in Tchernichowsky's own time.

Shaddai: "When Abram was ninety-nine years old, the Lord appeared to Abram and said to him: 'I am El Shaddai. Walk in My ways and be blameless (Gen. 17:1).'" Modern scholars believe the divine name to have its origins in the Akkadian *shadu*, "a mountain," which corresponds to the Hebrew divine epithet, *tsur*, "The Rock."